Strategic Studies Institute
and
U.S. Army War College Press

OPERATIONALIZING COUNTER
THREAT FINANCE STRATEGIES

Shima D. Keene

December 2014

*****

Comments pertaining to this report are invited and should be forwarded to: Director, Strategic Studies Institute and U.S. Army War College Press, U.S. Army War College, 47 Ashburn Drive, Carlisle, PA 17013-5010.

*****

This manuscript was funded by the U.S. Army War College External Research Associates Program. Information on this program is available on our website, *www.StrategicStudies Institute.army.mil*, at the Opportunities tab.

*****

*****

The Strategic Studies Institute and U.S. Army War College Press publishes a monthly email newsletter to update the national security community on the research of our analysts, recent and forthcoming publications, and upcoming conferences sponsored by the Institute. Each newsletter also provides a strategic commentary by one of our research analysts. If you are interested in receiving this newsletter, please subscribe on the SSI website at *www.StrategicStudiesInstitute.army.mil/newsletter*.

FOREWORD

It is a well established axiom that attempting to defeat an insurgency or a terrorist organization head-on is merely treating the symptoms of a problem. For long-term success, the campaign must also address the root causes of the insecurity that spawned conflict in the first place.

In this monograph, British academic and practitioner Dr. Shima Keene describes a number of ways in which financial intelligence can be leveraged not only to disrupt adversary activities, but also to provide indicators and warnings of future actions and, ultimately, to address underlying insecurities. Dr. Keene was previously both a banker and a British Army reservist. In this monograph, she uses her expertise as a threat finance specialist to outline specific areas where financial intelligence analysis techniques, which are common in the private sector, can be applied to combating insurgency, terrorism, and other hard security threats.

Dr. Keene argues that financial disruption techniques used in counterinsurgency have been poorly coordinated and at times counterproductive, and cites the targeting of the *Hawala* money transfer system as a specific example. Instead, she notes intelligence derived from analysis of financial data can provide much greater value in both understanding and predicting the adversary's activities, as well as providing for precise targeting to disrupt them.

The Strategic Studies Institute recommends this monograph not only to counterinsurgency and counterterrorism practitioners and policymakers, but also to the Intelligence community more widely; all of these will find its conclusions on the handling of financial data and the value of threat finance analysis valuable.

DOUGLAS C. LOVELACE, JR.
Director
Strategic Studies Institute and
    U.S. Army War College Press

ABOUT THE AUTHOR

SHIMA D. KEENE is a Director of the Conflict Studies Research Centre, Oxford as well as Director of the Security Economics Programme at the Institute for Statecraft, London, United Kingdom (UK). She is also a Deployable Civilian Expert (DCE) and a member of the UK government's Civilian Stabilisation Group (CSG) specializing in Intelligence and Security Sector Reform which sits under the Security and Justice Function of the CSG. She is a former Senior Research Fellow and Advisor at the Advanced Research and Assessment Group, UK Defence Academy, and Special Advisor to the UK Ministry of Defence (MoD), where she had responsibility for assessment and recommendations for the development of financial counterinsurgency (COIN) strategies in Afghanistan.

Dr. Keene advises and works closely with a number of British and international organizations on topics relating to national and international security including the MoD, various UK government departments and law enforcement agencies, the Organization for Security and Co-operation in Europe (OSCE), the Council of Europe, Global Futures Forum, the North Atlantic Treaty Organization (NATO), U.S. government departments and law enforcement agencies and various global private sector organizations. Dr. Keene has 25 years of practitioner experience in a number of industries including finance, defense, security, and telecommunications in both the public and private sectors, working with government departments, law enforcement, telecommunications and finance. She is also a former British Army reservist with 7 years military service, most of which was spent with 4th Battalion, the Parachute Regiment. Dr. Keene has published numerous internal and external MoD and NATO reports as well as award winning academic journal articles, and is the author of *Threat Finance: Disconnecting the Lifeline of Organized Crime and Terrorism* (Aldershot, UK: Ashgate, 2012). Dr. Keene graduated with honors from the University of Buckingham in Business Studies; and holds an MPhil in Defence and Security Studies from Cranfield University, Defence College of Management and Technology (formerly Royal Military College of Science), Defence Academy of the United Kingdom; and a Ph.D. in international criminal law from the Institute of Advanced Legal Studies, University of London.

SUMMARY

U.S. military leaders, planners, and decisionmakers face a new security environment in the 21st century, characterized by its complex networked nature, which has emerged as a result of globalization accompanied by the ever increasing speed of technological advancements. This in turn has created a new set of security dynamics that is increasingly spawning a variety of asymmetric threats, changing the very nature of conflict. The result is a complex and untidy security environment, where even attempting to define the nature of the threat has become difficult. Historically, adversaries were well-defined, allowing a relatively clear course of action to be chosen against them. This is no longer the case, as nonstate actors forming a global network of terrorist organizations, associated criminal groups, corrupt governments, and indifferent or uninformed individuals or corporations, increasingly take center stage. The state now faces an enemy whose asymmetry is such that concepts such as "civilian" and "military" or even "legality" have become obsolete.

The consequence is that the traditional approach of attempting to find a solution for a particular security problem has become ineffective. In fact, it is no longer appropriate to look for a single solution as such. In the new networked world, most problems are multidimensional in nature making them difficult or impossible to solve due to their incomplete, contradictory, and constantly evolving nature. These are generally referred to as "wicked" problems, characterized by their complex interdependencies where action taken to address one aspect of the problem may reveal or create additional problems.

As such, it is essential that a problem is examined not as a stand-alone subject, but in the context of the existing interdependencies so as to be better able to appreciate the possible knock-on effects of actions which may be taken. Furthermore, these challenges can no longer be tackled by any single organization or country. The hybrid nature of problems and conflict itself, coupled with resource limitations, will require partners to work more closely together than ever before. This multi-stakeholder environment in itself can be challenging due to the existence of differing cultures, both organizational and geographical, as well as differing perspectives and motives, despite the united goal of the partnership as a whole.

The reality of this threat environment is that it has changed the nature of warfare itself, with significant implications for the U.S. Army. In recent years, the role of the military has evolved from pure "warfighting" to more non-warfighting missions such as peace keeping and preventive engagements. These additional requirements demand that military personnel become more aware of the broader security picture, as well as that they develop additional skills that will allow them not only to be good soldiers, but to have the flexibility and adaptability to play a number of additional roles to include peacekeeper, humanitarian agent, law enforcement official, and diplomat, as the situation demands.

As such, it is important not only to know what the immediate problem is, but to understand the wider surrounding issues, as well as the underlying causes of that problem. Actions taken without an understanding of the full dynamics of the threat can backfire, and numerous examples are available from the last decade of counterinsurgency operations. Uninformed actions, however well-intentioned, will have negative side effects, and consequences potentially of sufficient magnitude to endanger the overall military mission.

This must be avoided at all costs. This monograph therefore provides recommendations for addressing a specific area where the capability of the United States and allied militaries can be augmented for the purpose of targeted action against adversaries: that of threat finance, and effective counter threat finance strategies.

OPERATIONALIZING COUNTER THREAT FINANCE STRATEGIES

INTRODUCTION – THE CHALLENGES

U.S. military leaders, planners, and decisionmakers face a new security environment in the 21st century, characterized by its complex networked nature, which has emerged as a result of globalization accompanied by the ever increasing speed of technological advancements. This in turn has created a new set of security dynamics that is increasingly spawning a variety of asymmetric threats, changing the very nature of conflict.

The result is a complex and untidy security environment, where even attempting to define the nature of the threat has become difficult. Historically, adversaries were well-defined, allowing a relatively clear course of action to be chosen against them. This is no longer the case, as nonstate actors forming a global network of terrorist organizations, associated criminal groups, corrupt governments, and indifferent or uninformed individuals or corporations, increasingly take center stage. The state now faces an enemy whose asymmetry is such that concepts such as civilian and military or even legality have become obsolete.[1]

The consequence is that the traditional approach of attempting to find a solution for a particular security problem has become ineffective. In fact, it is no longer appropriate to look for a single solution as such. This is because in the new networked world, most problems are multidimensional in nature. This makes the problems difficult or impossible to solve due to their incomplete, contradictory, and constantly evolving nature.[2] These are generally referred to as "wicked" problems which are characterized by their complex interdependencies, where action taken to address one aspect of the problem may reveal or create additional problems.

As such, it is essential that the problem is examined not as a stand-alone subject, but in the context of the existing interdependencies in order to be able to appreciate better the possible knock-on effects of actions which may be taken. Furthermore, these challenges can no longer be tackled by any single organization or country. The hybrid nature of problems and conflict itself coupled with resource limitations will require partners to work more closely together than ever before. This multistakeholder environment in itself can be challenging due to the existence of differing cultures, both organizational and geographical, as well as differing perspectives and motives, despite the united goal of the partnership as a whole.

The reality of this threat environment is that it has changed the nature of warfare itself, with significant implications for the U.S. Army. In recent years, the role of the military has evolved from pure warfighting to more non-warfighting missions such as peacekeeping and preventive engagements. These additional requirements require military personnel to become more aware of the broader security picture, as well as to develop additional skills that will allow them not only to be good soldiers, but to have the flexibility and adaptability to play a number of additional roles to include peacekeeper, humanitarian agent, law enforcement official, and diplomat, as the situation demands.

As such, it is important not only to know what the immediate problem is, but to understand the wider surrounding issues, as well as the underlying causes of that problem. Action taken without an understanding of the full dynamics of the threat can backfire, and numerous examples are available from the last decade of counterinsurgency (COIN) operations. Uninformed actions, however well-intentioned, will have negative side effects, and consequences potentially of sufficient magnitude to endanger the overall military mission.

This must be avoided at all costs. This monograph therefore provides recommendations for addressing a specific area where the capability of U.S. and allied militaries can be augmented for the purpose of targeted action against adversaries: that of threat finance, and effective counter threat finance strategies.

THE ROOT CAUSES OF INSECURITY AND CONFLICT

In order to provide context for these recommendations, we need to consider the unstable and conflict-prone environments in which they could be employed. Many of the factors that cause insecurity and conflict, such as terrorism and insurgencies, are not new. Insurgencies of the kind witnessed in the early 21st century have forerunners in many parts of the world throughout human history. Early examples of the potentially catastrophic effects of insurgency are the invasion of the Akkadian empire in Mesopotamia in the 22nd century BC by the Gutians ("barbarian people") from the Zagros Mountains, which resulted in the eventual collapse of the empire; and insurgency operations conducted by a variety of barbarians such as the Huns,[3] which contributed to the fall of the Roman empire in the 5th century AD.[4] Other examples include the Peninsular War (1807-14), for the control of the Iberian Peninsula, which led to the defeat of Napoleon in 1814, and the Greek war for independence against the Ottomans in the 19th century (1821-32). Importantly, some of the key drivers of insurgencies remain unchanged over time and therefore can be used as indicators and warnings of future instability.

Similarly, terrorism has served as one of the most common expressions of man's inhumanity to man since time immemorial. Although definitions remain controversial, the term "terrorism" is generally used to refer to the killing of innocent people[5] with most accepting the United Nations (UN) description as:

> . . . any act intended to cause death or serious bodily harm to civilians or non-combatants with the purpose of intimidating or compelling a government or an international organization to do or abstain from doing any act.[6]

Early examples of terrorism include the terror attacks by the Cimbri tribe in 105 BC which led Rome to declare a state of emergency known as *terror cimbricus*[7], or the use of the word by Jacobins imposing a reign of terror during the French Revolution in the 18th century. However, it was the events of September 11, 2001 (9/11) that brought terrorism to the top of the political agenda for the United States and its allies. The events of 9/11 served as a turning point for terrorism, highlighting its metamorphosis into a new age of international terrorism, marked by different motivations, actors, and sponsors. In addition, greater ambitions and lethality were highlighted, no longer confined by geographical boundaries, representing an upward shift to a new level of global threat previously unseen and unknown. As such, not only will the need for effective counterterrorism and COIN doctrine continue into the foreseeable future, but counter efforts will need to be more sophisticated than ever before to tackle this new form of adversary at all levels.

However, attempting to defeat an insurgency or a terrorist organization head-on is merely treating the symptoms of a problem. For long-term success, the military campaign must also address the root causes of that insecurity. In order to achieve this, a move away from a pure focus on tactical COIN and counterterrorism operations is essential. Instead, a comprehensive approach that combines economic, governance, and security measures should be adopted, where the understanding of threat finance should play a key part. This can be better achieved when the reasons of insecurity and conflict are fully understood. Numerous factors contribute to instability, insecurity, and conflict, ranging from the disruptive influences of adversary organizations, such as terrorist networks and organized crime groups (OCGs), to political unrest and social revolution. Some of the key contributors are as follows.

Bad Governance.

Bad governance is a major cause of instability and conflict. Inadequate governments rife with incompetence, coupled with the lack of an effective judicial system, promote a culture that lacks transparency and accountability. This in turn creates an environment where corruption and criminality can prosper. Money and power are key motivations. In addition, social pressures, especially those created by rapid increases in population density, can lead to instabilities of governance. This results in general insecurity and instability as even established governments are overtaken by rapid and drastic change as they fail to cope with explosive social pressures, causing breakdown of social stability and increased mobility. The result is a failed state.[8]

Failed and Failing States.

Failed states are one of the dominant and defining features of conflict. States that cannot adapt to the changing global context risk collapse, and many such failures will be accompanied by substantial outbreaks of violence. Furthermore, poor governance, economic deprivation, and inequality that characterize failed and failing states are likely to spread to neighboring states in the form of economic migration as well as crime.[9]

Economic Resources.

Competition over primary resources such as energy, food, minerals, and water has played a key role in conflict throughout human history. Economic resources will continue to drive states' security interests in terms of both control of those resources and methods of their distribution.[10] In addition, these considerations are likely to dictate why we fight, where we fight, as well as how we fight. This competition also engenders a sense of injustice which may lead to eventual confrontation.

Inequality.

The injustices felt as a result of uneven distribution of wealth will contribute to conflict. This wealth gap sets the rich against the poor, both within countries (especially in developing countries) and between countries, making some national borders especially sensitive. The degree of sensitivity and potential problems can be expressed in the ratio of wealth differential. For example, the ratio between the United States and Mexico is 6:1. In other words, each U.S. citizen is on average six times wealthier than each Mexican. Similarly, the wealth ratio for Spain and Algeria is 14:1.[11] This disparity results in economic migrants entering the European Union (EU), causing further friction.

Inability to Manage Change.

One of the biggest causes of drastic instability is the failure of societies to handle change. Excessive conservatism and resistance to change, especially when this is forced upon a population, causes tensions to build within society, just as seismic tension does in California's San Andreas Fault. If the accumulated tensions are released suddenly, the result can be catastrophic.

Information Ubiquity.

As a result of the internet and the availability and affordability of technologies such as mobile phones or personal computers, populations are able to access a wide range of information quickly. Such ubiquity of information is essential to sustain the vast urbanized populations, but it also brings with it new forms of power that we must understand in order to be able to exploit and to counter them, as well as to integrate them with other forms of power. Failure to do so will result in instabilities and loss of influence and power for governments and established political structures.

Extremist Nonstate Actors.

International terrorist organizations such as al-Qaeda and its associates are likely to remain a significant threat to the United States and its allies. In its globalized franchised form, these actors create partnerships with local militants and organized criminality. Together, they take advantage of any emerging instability which they will exploit as a weapon against the West.

Ideology, Culture, and Religion.

Ideological movements, based on religion and identity, will remain a significant factor as people continue to fight for their beliefs. Irreconcilable cultural and religious differences, between and within communities, local, regional, virtual (cyber) and international will continue to be a destabilizing factor. Furthermore, the spread of ideology has no geographic constraints due to advancements in communications technologies.

Conclusion.

Any one of these factors can cause conflict. However, the more factors present, the more likely it is that conflict will emerge, and the more complex and intractable will be any resulting problems. Many of these factors are driven or exacerbated by financial/ economic concerns. In addition, the nature and impact of the current global economic and social revolution will dictate where conflict is most likely to happen, and where the U.S. military should be ready to deploy and employ its tools of influence.

CONFLICT AS A NECESSARY EVIL

At the same time, instability and friction, along with growth and decline, are essential components of a viable society. This is because it is only when existing practices are challenged that growth is possible. Unfortunately, change is never universally welcomed, nor is it necesssarily good, and a degree of conflict is therefore inevitable. Therefore, the key is to ensure that the resulting conflict does not escalate out of control. To this end, it is imperative to be able to determine what level of instability is beneficial and sustainable for a society and to assess when that level becomes too high or too low. In addition, when instability becomes unmanageable, it is important to assess accurately what action is necessary to bring the situation back under control.

This can only be achieved by obtaining appropriate intelligence in order to assess correctly the precise nature of the threats, instabilies, and opportunities present in any given situation. Financial intelligence plays a key part in not only assessing the level of instability, but also in suggesting ways to bring instability back under control. This is where threat finance comes into play.

WHAT IS THREAT FINANCE?

Threat finance is the means and methods used by the adversary to ensure their economic survival. The term "adversary" refers to individuals and organizations that pose a threat to national and international security, including, but not limited to, a wide range of actors such as terrorist organizations, narco- and human traffickers, transnational organized crime groups, and cyber criminals. Put simply, threat finance is how bad guys make, hide, move, and spend their money. Understanding threat finance means understanding the various mechanisms and networks of third parties that enable that to happen.

Adversaries engage in a wide variety of activities, both legitimate and illegitimate, to secure their cash flow and to maintain their assets. Activities to that aim include kidnapping, extortion, arms dealing, drug dealing, human trafficking, counterfeiting, cyber-crime, and fraud. Legitimate activities include businesses and financial investment such as financial securities trading, as well as other types of investments in commodities and real estate. Where the sources of funding are illegitimate, money laundering occurs in an effort to make the money appear legitimate to conceal its criminal origins. The instruments for money laundering are extensive and include the abuse of shell companies, mortgages, insurance products, precious stones, real estate, high value goods, charities, and banks.[12]

Counter threat finance (CTF), on the other hand, refers to activities intended to undermine those threats. This is typically achieved through the use of financial intelligence and a number of other available measures such as asset seizures, economic sanctions, and anti-money laundering regimes. The stakeholders of CTF are broad, ranging from governments, law enforcement, and the military to the private sector, to include banks, insurance companies, mortgage lenders, money service businesses (MSBs), law firms, accountancy firms, and real estate agents.

Financial intelligence is at the heart of CTF strategies, even though the terms "threat finance" and "financial intelligence" are often used interchangeably.

In addition, the definition of both terms can appear ambiguous due to their dynamic nature. This should not be seen as a negative, as it is the fluid nature of these tools that will prove to serve well against the equally ambiguous threat environment outlined at the beginning of this monograph. As such, financial intelligence and the use of CTF strategies will be critical in unravelling the complexity of the threats that reveal themselves through financial networks.

FINANCIAL INTELLIGENCE

The use of financial intelligence in defense has improved in recent years, but nevertheless remains rudimentary compared to the analysis provided in the private sector, such as by investment banks. Its use in defense also displays a tendency to over focus on individual strands or components of finance. Although "following the money" is a key part of developing financial intelligence, this alone is not enough. It is only the starting point. What really matters is the interpretation of the data so that the intelligence gathered can be used to help achieve a given objective. In other words, the key is in the analysis of what that financial raw intelligence actually means, and how it can be used.

Thus the same principle applies to financial intelligence as to intelligence in general. A common mistake is to consider "intelligence" as being synonymous with "information." However, information by itself is not intelligence. Information plus analysis equals intelligence. So without analysis, there is no intelligence. Misuse of the term has also led to the phrase "collecting intelligence" instead of "collecting information." Intelligence is not what is collected; it is what is produced after collected data is evaluated and analyzed. While this should to be a basic principle of established intelligence disciplines, its application in the field of financial intelligence is even more insufficient than in other areas of intelligence assessments.

Furthermore, this analysis requires thoughtful contemplation that results in conclusions and recommendations. Computers may assist with analysis by compiling large amounts of data into an easily accessible format, but this is still only collated data; it is not analyzed data or information, and, as such, falls far short of being intelligence.

The same applies to financial intelligence in that even when valuable financial data is collected, the mere collation of such information is in itself not altogether helpful. The value is in the interpretation, without which CTF strategies cannot be operationalized fully. The significance and its relevance to the military is that the correct interpretation can be used to reveal patterns of enemy behavior, motivations and possible intentions as well as lifestyles and networks, all of which will impact directly upon military operations within a COIN environment.

After all, money is in itself just paper or coins. What makes money so important to people is its ability to transform into power, lifestyle, influence, food, shelter, weapons, a wife (or more than one in some cultures), family, realization of dreams, and more. In other words, it is the corresponding economic value as opposed its mere financial value that is at stake. As such, money, or financial intelligence, must be understood within its broader economic context.

SECURITY ECONOMICS

Threat finance is a component of security economics which is the analysis of the economic aspects of human-induced insecurity, such as terrorism and organized crime. Many security threats are driven by the desire for economic gain, either as an end in itself, or to assist in achieving an ultimate end. In other cases, economic factors can be used to determine likely future human actions. For example, the decision for an individual to join either the Taliban or the Afghan army is often based on economic factors as opposed to ideology alone. There are undoubtedly individuals with strong beliefs that will not be swayed by economic factors. However, for the majority, the ability to survive economically will be the main factor.

This equally applies to the wide network of individuals in the financial network that enable threat finance to take place, referring for example to individuals who work in the financial system who may be willing to turn a blind eye to certain customers for personal economic gain, especially if the risk is considered to be minimal. For example, a mortgage salesman may be willing to turn a blind eye to certain risks in order to meet his monthly sales target. Internal policy and the existence of internal compliance officers are of limited effectiveness in deterring such activity when economic motivations override ethical considerations. As such, the broader economic considerations must be part of any CTF strategy.

BRIEF HISTORY OF THREAT FINANCE

The concept of threat finance originated from terrorist finance. The events of 9/11 not only brought terrorism to the top of the political agenda for the United States and its allies, but highlighted the importance of tackling terrorist finance, which was acknowledged as being the lifeblood of terrorism. It was recognized that by disrupting the terrorist funding supply chain, it was possible to mitigate and maybe even prevent further terrorist attacks.[13]

However, as the interest in terrorist finance intensified, so too did the realization of its complexity. Furthermore, as the depth of understanding increased, it became clear that the subject of terrorist finance could not be looked at in isolation. It is this realization that gave birth to the term "threat finance" which examines not only terrorist finance, but also other strands of threat finances, referring to the finances of a wide range of adversaries to include terrorist organizations, narco- and human traffickers, transnational organized crime groups, and cyber criminals.

CTF EFFORTS TO DATE

Following the 9/11 attacks, the first financial strike by the United States in the so-called "global war on terror" came in the form of Executive Order 13224,[14] which targeted the financial assets of organizations and individuals linked to terrorism, including al-Qaeda. Executive Order 13224 was followed by numerous initiatives by the United States, the United Kingdom (UK), and various international bodies creating many new organizations with the goal of attacking terrorist financial networks. These multilateral initiatives led to the designation of 315 entities and seizures amounting to $200 million (£106 million)[15] in monetary and other assets in over 1,400 accounts worldwide, as well as the arrests of over 4,000 suspects,[16] including many senior al-Qaeda operatives, making the countering of terrorist finance one of the most active dimensions in the global war on terror.

The events of 9/11 also led to increased international cooperation. Over 100 countries have offered increased intelligence support leading to intensified counterterrorist operations by more than 200 intelligence and security services worldwide.[17] In addition, at the Asia-Pacific Economic Cooperation Forum (APEC) Summit in Shanghai, China, in October 2001, APEC leaders issued a statement on counterterrorism in which they strongly condemned the 9/11 attacks and pledged to improve counterterrorism cooperation through a number of means.

These means have included putting in place appropriate financial measures to prevent the flow of funds to terrorists, including work on combating financial crimes through the APEC Finance Ministers Working Group on Fighting Financial Crime, as well as more involvement in related international standard setting regimes. These initiatives have led to agreements to undertake early and constructive consultation prior to designating terrorist assets, exchanging information on national legal criteria required to freeze terrorist funds, and updating global assessments of frozen terrorists' funds. However, the stakeholders of CTF are not restricted to governments, militaries, and the law enforcement community but extend to the private sector.

PRIVATE SECTOR

The aim of CTF in general is to create a financial environment that is hostile to adversary organizations. With that in mind, governments and regulators are continuing to introduce new laws and regulations to keep up to pace with the ever mutating *modus operandi* of individuals involved in threat finance. The requirement to comply covers not only financial institutions, but also other organizations such as estate agents, legal firms, and accounting firms. Together, the private sector can be described as being the first line of defense for CTF strategy and operations. At the heart of the Anti-Money Laundering (AML) regimes is the concept to "Know Your Customer" (KYC) and the submission of Suspicious Activity Reports (SARs), both of which are rich sources of financial intelligence.

Know Your Customer.

The KYC requirement is essentially the due diligence procedures which should be carried out as part of the initial client acceptance procedures. These include the verification of identity through the presentation of personal identification documentation such as a passport, supported by utility bills to verify the address of the potential customer. Other risk factors to be taken into consideration include the geographical location of the client (whether this is categorized as a high-risk country), as well as whether the client is registered as a politically exposed person (PEP), a term describing someone who has been entrusted with a prominent public function, or an individual who is closely related to such a person. Examples include current or former senior officials in the executive, legislative, administrative, military, or judicial branch of a foreign government (elected or not); a senior executive of a foreign government-owned commercial enterprise; being a corporation, business, or other entity formed by or for the benefit of any such individual; an immediate family member of such an individual; or any individual known to be a close personal or professional associate.

PEPs generally present a higher risk for potential involvement in bribery and corruption by virtue of their position and the influence that they may hold. As such, they are more closely monitored for the purpose of CTF activities. The purpose of monitoring financial transactions is so that any unexplained or potentially suspicious activity can be reported to the Financial Intelligence Unit (FIU) of that country.

Suspicious Activity Reports (SARs).

A SAR is a report submitted by organizations such as financial institutions to include banks, mortgage providers, and insurance companies, as well as real estate agents, law firms, and accounting firms, to report suspicious or potentially suspicious financial activity to the FIU. Each jurisdiction has its own FIU. For example, the Financial Crimes Enforcement Network (FinCEN), which is a bureau of the U.S. Department of the Treasury, is the FIU for the United States. Its equivalent (in terms of its role as the country's FIU) in the UK is the National Crime Agency (NCA), which is a law enforcement agency.

SARs include detailed information about financial transactions that are, or appear to be suspicious. Reporting institutions are required to categorize these transactions as either potential money laundering or terrorist financing activity. The FIU collates the SARs received and makes the reports available to regional law enforcement agencies based on the geographical location of the account holder. It is a requirement in the UK that all financial institutions have a system in place to monitor financial transactions and to report any suspicious activity to the FIU.[18]

The first stage of the risk-based financial monitoring process begins with financial profiling. Financial profiling takes into consideration factors such as age, profession, known income, and expenditure. Other factors such as peer group analysis are used to set parameters indicating normal activity. Financial transactions are then monitored using the rules derived from the financial profiles. Any transactions that fall outside these "normal" parameters flag up an alert which is subsequently investigated by one of the bank's specialist financial investigators.

SARs can provide an essential pool of financial intelligence and place the private sector in the forefront of the fight against terrorism and crime. SARs, also known as disclosures, contribute intelligence to existing law enforcement operations, identify the proceeds of crime, and initiate investigation into previously unknown criminal activities. Unusual or suspicious activities can also be identified not only through the monitoring of transactions, but also through monitoring customer contacts, such as meetings, discussions, and in-country visits, as well as third party information such as newspapers, the internet, and vendor databases. Knowledge of the client's environment in terms of an understanding of the political situation in his home country may further contribute to its analysis.

SMART SANCTIONS

Existing CTF measures which target specific individuals and organizations responsible or associated with the funding of terrorism can be described as falling under the category of "smart sanctions."[19] The origin of smart/targeted sanctions predates the events of 9/11. A brief background may be helpful in understanding the concept which led to its development. Prior to the existence of smart sanctions, the use of standard economic sanctions against enemy states, including those which supported terrorism, was commonplace. However, traditional economic sanctions have long been recognized as being ineffective. In addition, they possess a highly undesirable side effect in the form of an indiscriminate impact on a country, which can entail severe negative humanitarian consequences for the civilian population.[20]

This side effect is particularly of concern in the context of terrorism. International terrorism frequently utilizes the suffering of innocent civilian populations in two ways. First, the victimhood of those people is emphasized, either to the victims themselves or to those who empathize with those individuals. The goal is to radicalize those individuals so that they can either be recruited into the terrorist organizations or provide other means of support.

Second, examples of unjust treatment are used to attract funding, which in turn is used for the purpose of financing terrorism. This is of particular importance, because the origin of much of the donor funding is derived through appealing to the charitable nature of wealthy individuals who may or may not be aware of the ultimate purpose of their financial donations.[21]

WHAT COUNTER THREAT FINANCE STRATEGIES CAN DO

The targeting of the financial, and perhaps more importantly, the economic base of an organization, will not only impact the operational capability of that organization, but can ultimately lead to its destruction. To date, CTF strategies have been used predominantly for the purpose of disruption. However, the potential application of CTF strategies goes far wider. They have the potential to be a multifaceted weapon, capable of tackling a number of issues relevant to the military not only in terms of enemy disruption, but for detecting impending instability.

For example, at a macro level, the movement of money has the ability to provide early warning signals of impending activity. If people (especially key individuals and organizations who possess the best local knowledge) are moving their money and assets to another country, this could signify expectancy of future instability with potential security implications. Furthermore, if financial/economic migration intensifies sharply, this could be catastrophic for the region in itself, as the mass migration of money may cause economic collapse, again leading to social unrest.

In such situations, it would be the role of the international community to intervene to provide financial assistance to stabilize the economic situation. Although the military would not be involved in this stage of the process, this is an unstable situation which could easily escalate with numerous security implications of direct relevance to the military. As such, intelligence assessments of these warning signs should be observed and tracked carefully by military planners.

Similarly at a micro level, the movement of money can signify impending action, or equally important, inaction by adversary organizations allowing the military to plan its own operations accordingly. Here, the proverb attributed to both Napoleon and Frederick the Great that "an army marches on its stomach" ("*C'est la soupe qui fait le soldat*") translated as the "soup makes the soldier," stands true. The proverb suggests that a group of soldiers or workers can only fight or function effectively if they have been well fed.[22] What is needed to feed soldiers is, of course, money to buy the food. In addition to the food of the proverb, soldiers or insurgents depend for effective fighting ability on shelter or accommodation, logistic support for movement, medical services to treat the injured, and supplies of weapons and ammunition. In addition, money is also needed to buy loyalty and increase morale, as well as care for the relatives of the soldiers/insurgents in the event that they do not survive a battle, and leave family behind that require support.

Therefore, when payments are delayed or not made, the entire logistical supply chain of the essentials of food and other vital supplies becomes disrupted, impacting heavily on the physical and psychological state of those fighters. This, in turn, will affect not only their ability, but also their motivation and willingness to fight. As such, financial intelligence is able to serve as a good indicator of the level of morale, as well as the combat capability of the insurgents.

Although more work has been achieved in this field at a local level (in country), there are additional upstream factors that impact upon local circumstances, which also need to be taken into consideration. It is also important to understand the various sources of financial information that can be used to produce financial intelligence for this purpose.

SOURCES OF FINANCIAL INFORMATION

Financial intelligence is the end product of analysis of information gathered about the financial affairs of individuals or entities of interest. It has the ability to complement existing intelligence by providing additional supporting evidence, as well as to provide new leads or to detect activities or networks which were previously unknown.

Raw financial data can be obtained from a variety of sources in the private and public sectors as well as from individuals. Examples in the private sector include those financial institutions and service providers already listed, as well as MSBs such as Western Union or Informal Value Transfer Services (IVTS). It is worth noting that there is a wealth of data not currently utilized which falls outside the previously mentioned SARs. Many banks, for example, have the mechanisms in place to enable them to monitor and detect not only the financial transactions themselves, but also where the money is coming from, where it is going, changes of address, contact numbers, and so forth.

However, it should also be noted that the private sector is not an unlimited resource. Such organizations are bound by laws and regulations as well as internal policies, and client data is protected by data protection and human rights legislation. However, if the questions are framed correctly and the organizations are approached in the right way, it is possible to access this data which can be extremely valuable.

Although the monitoring and reporting requirements mentioned earlier relate to the regulated sector, this does not mean that the unregulated sector also does not hold valuable financial intelligence. IVTS such as *Hawala*[23] retain transactional data which can be highly relevant.[24] The challenge is that due to the lack of standardization,[25] some of the information made be difficult to interpret without the help of the *Hawaladar*.[26] Furthermore, as there is no regulatory requirement for holding onto data, historic transactions may be discarded, once the business has concluded (i.e., the financial transaction has been made), and it is entirely at the *Hawaladar's* discretion how long he wishes to maintain records.[27]

Financial information can also be provided by various private sector organizations where the core business is not financial. Examples include retail outlets such as supermarket chains that provide loyalty cards. Such information is particularly useful in that the stores often offer a variety of services to include insurance, communications (mobile phones, landline phones and internet), as well as financing, all of which is a rich source of financial information. In addition, the stores' delivery services for many items such as food, furniture, and electrical goods, provide valuable data in terms of addresses connected to the account holder. Airline companies, utility providers such as electricity or gas, mobile telephone and broadband providers, and mail delivery companies also provide valuable financial information as well as additional information such as telephone numbers and addresses.

M-transfers, also referred to as mobile money, mobile money transfer, and mobile wallet, generally refer to payment services made via a mobile device such as a mobile phone. Instead of paying with cash, check, or credit cards, a consumer can use a mobile phone to pay for a wide range of services, as well as for digital or hard goods. Such services have become increasingly popular and widespread, especially in developing countries, where the formal banking system may be limited or nonexistent. This forms a relatively new method of moving money or paying for goods, in that the technology that is needed, namely a mobile device and connection to the internet, have only been in existence since the late-1990s.[28]

In addition to M-transfers, on-line auction houses such as EBay and Amazon can also provide valuable sources of financial information.[29] Although their purpose and use is predominantly legitimate, as with the *Hawala* system, there is on-going concern as to possible use for criminality due to inadequate regulations and loopholes in the law, which has diluted the requirement to report suspicious transactions. Also, even where regulations exist, since they were developed with bank transactions in mind they do little to cater to M-transactions which are typically small value high volume transactions.

In addition, there are challenges in terms of how long records of transactions are required to be kept. Nevertheless, it must be recognized that this is potentially a good source of financial information which could be utilized. Furthermore, it is likely that as with any emerging technology or service, regulations will be enhanced once the dangers of not doing so are further recognized.

Financial intelligence can also be obtained from public sector sources such as government departments dealing with tax and social benefits. It is also important to understand the ways in which illegitimate money flows are moved. For this, an appreciation of money laundering and of the various vehicles used to launder money are necessary.

Money Laundering.

Much of existing counter threat finance strategies relies upon existing anti-money laundering (AML) regimes enforced by legislation and regulation. However, there are two main challenges to this approach. The first is that the AML regimes were initially introduced in the 1990s in response to the laundering of the proceeds of narcotics trafficking related money.[30] Although the AML regimes have been modified to include other aspects of threat finance, such as terrorist finance, critics argue that this has simply been an "add-on" which fails to tackle the issue of terrorist financing appropriately.[31] The existing approach is better described as being "one size fits all" as opposed to a tailored approach to tackle finances relating to terrorism. Nevertheless, the main benefit of the AML regimes is that financial information is captured, which can then be interrogated by the investigating authorities.[32]

A further challenge is that money laundering is understood by many simply as a process whereby "bad" money turns into "good" money.[33] Unfortunately, money does not only come in two simple shades of black and white. White money, also known as clean money, refers to "ordinary" money that is obtained in small denominations through hard work and related bonuses, prudent investment, or inheritance.[34] The opposite of clean money is dirty or "black" money, which is obtained through criminal means. But there is also "grey" money, money that the owner wishes to disassociate him or herself from, even though its origins may not have been illegal.

One example is where an individual may not wish his spouse, partner, or relatives to be aware of his wealth for a variety of reasons, such as impending divorce. Another example is where a profitable business may wish to maintain a low profile to avoid attracting attention which may result in increased competition.[35] In addition, there is "hot" money, referring to financial movements stimulated by adverse changes in economic, social, and/or political conditions. A further consideration is that the best place to hide black money is with white or grey money, and the movements are often made unnecessarily complex in an attempt by the criminal to put off the investigator as a result of the lack of transparency, as well as the time needed to unravel the financial audit trail.

HOW EFFECTIVE HAS CTF BEEN TO DATE?

The importance of tackling the finances of adversary organizations has long been recognized. However, despite the existence of relevant legislation and regulation, the current environment continues to favor the adversary. For example, some economists have calculated that less than 1 percent of terrorist finances have been captured to date.[36] There are many reasons for this, but one is because of limited understanding as to what threat finance is in terms of first, how to detect it, and second, knowing what to do about it. Although the understanding of each of the individual components of threat finance has undeniably increased in recent years, counter threat finance strategies have not been particularly effective in real terms.

One reason is in relation to the way in which CTF strategies are understood and applied. The understanding of the subject is often limited and over-simplistic and, as such, has not been fit for the purpose. In addition, finance is often treated as a stand-alone subject. Instead, it should be treated not only as valuable intelligence in its own right, but also a tool that enables different types of intelligence to be brought together, and to validate or discard existing intelligence as appropriate. This is particularly relevant in an era where intelligence fusion is continuing to be recognized as key to the future of defense intelligence.

Lessons Not Learned.

Financial disruption strategies to date, typically characterized by their disjointed nature, have not been particularly effective. For example, in Afghanistan, in some cases efforts to disrupt Taliban finances are likely to have done more harm than good in terms of the overall COIN effort. A case in point is the pursuit of *Hawaladars,* an easy target, where the broader economic consequences of such actions are frequently overlooked. The disruption of a single *Hawaladar,* especially if the action is not justified, will do more to promote insurgency than to prevent it. In general, there is an overemphasis on disruption, where the goals are so focused that they frequently fail to acknowledge the damage that action might be causing in the wider context, which in turn exacerbates the underlying problem.

CONCLUSIONS

CTF strategies have the potential to become "hyper-strategic" weapons due to the fact that "financial war" is easily manipulated and allows for concealed actions, as well as having the capacity to be highly destructive. Furthermore, financial warfare is likely to be an increasing form of conflict due to its position which lies at the intersection of powerful long-term trends in technology, networks, information, and finance. The precise targeting feature of financial warfare, relative to conventional economic warfare, marks a significant change in the nature of conflict.

In addition, the use of finance should be recognized as a tool for influence. Financial intelligence holds special utility in that it is easily controlled to actionable outcomes designed to influence target behavior, the target being any individual or organization in the financial logistical supply chain. Influence is reliant on the successful manipulation of incentives and disincentives. This involves shaping the spectrum of options that are available to groups through tailored and focused activities aimed at specific pressure points.

However, in order to achieve this, there must be the willingness to embrace more complex financial analysis to include "high" finance. To date, there has been a tendency to overfocus on targeting the vast volume of low hanging fruit; the "smart" targeting of "low volume, high return" targets must also be encouraged. Given the constraints in available resources, every effort must be made to pursue actions that optimize return on investment. In order to further the U.S. Army's development and capability in effectively operationalizing CTF strategies in future years, the following recommendations should be considered.

FUTURE COUNTER THREAT FINANCE STRATEGIES: RECOMMENDATIONS FOR THE U.S. ARMY

1. **Integration**—Counter finance strategies should be fully integrated as part of a comprehensive COIN/CT/stabilization strategy, to ensure that short-, me-

dium-, and long-term financial targeting strategies are adopted to address both upstream and downstream finances to maximum effect.

2. **Embrace Complexity** — The willingness to embrace more complex high finance methods must be developed. In order to address the tendency to overfocus on targeting the vast volume of low hanging fruit, the smart targeting of "low volume, high return" targets must be encouraged.

3. **Influence** — The use of finance as a tool for influence should be further explored through developing knowledge of the broader financial network in order to be able to identify suitable pressure points.

4. **Knowledge and Intelligence Gaps** — These gaps should be addressed through education, the use of suitably qualified expertise, and by carrying out a self-assessment to ensure that the right questions are being framed, and that the right people are being engaged to obtain the necessary answers.

5. **Global Financial Audit Trail** — A deeper understanding of the broader global financial networks and investment strategies will help identify key vulnerabilities in the networks.

6. **Financial Intelligence** — Finances, including economic assets, should be viewed not only as a target subject to disruption, but also as a lucrative intelligence source. The existing tendency to focus on individual strands or components of finance should be avoided and replaced with a conscious effort to adopt a networked approach to the collection and analysis of financial data. Collation of financial data by following the money should be supported by better analysis to enable better use of that data. In other words, better interpretation of financial data focusing on possible application is needed. Appropriate financial analysis/

intelligence will reveal patterns of enemy behavior, motivations, possible intensions, lifestyles, networks, as well as morale and readiness to fight.

7. **Kinetic vs. Influence**—Caution should be exercised against the overuse of kinetic targeting. The impact of such action must first be properly assessed not only in terms of the enemy, but the wider network which will consist of both those who are part of the adversary network, as well as civilians who should not be regarded as collateral damage—either in a physical or a financial/economic sense. Instead, consideration should be given to the possibility of replacing kinetic action with influence strategies whenever possible.

8. *Hawala* **System**—Targeting the *Hawala* system, as well as associated *Hawaladars*, must be carried out with caution, taking local economic factors into consideration. Cultural considerations must form part of any finance targeting to enable effective disruption operations to take place while mitigating side effects.

ENDNOTES

1. Harold A. Gould and Franklin C. Spinney, *4GW is Here!* Center for South Asian Studies Newsletter, Charlottesville, VA: University of Virginia, 2001, available from *www.virginia.edu/soasia/newsletter/Fall01/warfare.html*, accessed on October 10, 2013; and *www.smallwarsjournal.com/documents/ 4gw.htm*, accessed on October 10, 2013.

2. Australian Government, "Tackling Wicked Problems: a Public Policy Perspective," Canberra, Australia: Australian Public Service Commission, 2007, available from *www.apsc.gov.au/ publications-and-media/archive/publications-archive/tackling-wicked-problems*, accessed on March 3, 2014.

3. Huns were a nomadic horse people migrating from Central Asia. They appeared in Europe around 370 AD and caused considerable harm to the Roman power in the West. See Max

Boot, *Invisible Armies: An Epic History of Guerrilla Warfare from Ancient Times to the Present*, New York and London, UK: Liveright Publishing Corporation, 2013, pp. 26-27.

4. *Ibid.*

5. Robert Mackay, "Can Soldiers be Victims of Terrorism?" *New York Times*, November 20, 2009.

6. United Nations Secretary General Report, November 2004.

7. Donald Greer, *The Incidence of the Terror during the French Revolution: A Statistician Interpretation*, Cambridge, MA: Harvard University Press, 1935.

8. Chris Donnelly and David McOwat, *Understanding the Revolution in the Nature of Conflict*, Global Perspective Statecraft Paper, October 23, 2012, available from *www.statecraft.org.uk/ research/understanding-revolution-nature-conflict www.statecraft.org*, accessed on April 19, 2014.

9. *The Future Character of Conflict*, London, UK: Ministry of Defence, available from *www.gov.uk/government/uploads/system/ uploads/attachment_data/file/33685/FCOCReadactedFinalWeb.pdf*, accessed on April 10, 2014.

10. Donnelly and McOwat, *Understanding the Revolution in the Nature of Conflict*.

11. Chris Donnelly and David McOwat, *Adapting Forces to Deal with New Challenges to National and International Security*, Global Perspective Statecraft Paper, October 18, 2012, available from *www.statecraft.org.uk/research/adapting-forces-deal-new-challenges- national-and-international-security*, accessed on April 19, 2014.

12. Shima D Keene, *Threat Finance: Disconnecting the Lifeline of Organized Crime and Terrorism*, Abingdon, UK: Gower Publishing, 2011, p. 162.

13. *Ibid.*, p. 5.

14. U.S. Department of the Treasury, Office of Foreign Assets Control, "Executive Order 13224, Blocking Property and Prohibiting Transactions with Persons who Commit, Threaten to Commit, or Support Terrorism," available from *www.treasury.gov/resource-center/sanctions/programs/documents/terror.pdf*, accessed on April 13, 2014.

15. Transnational Institute, "Global Enforcement Regimes Transnational Organized Crime, International Terrorism and Money Laundering," Report from the TNI Crime and Globalisation seminar, Amsterdam, The Netherlands, April 28-29, 2005, p. 20, available from *www.tni.org/sites/www.tni.org/archives/crime-docs/enforce.pdf*, accessed on April 13, 1014.

16. *Ibid.*

17. Dean C. Alexander and Yonah Alexander, *Terrorism and Business,* New York: Transnational Publishers Inc., 2002. p. 184.

18. Trifin J. Roule and Jeremy Kinsell, "Legislative and Bureaucratic Impediments to Suspicious Transaction Reporting Regimes," *Journal of Money Laundering Control,* Vol. 6, No. 2, 2002, p. 151.

19. An unrelated example current at the time of writing is the U.S. and Canadian sanctions against key individuals close to the Russian leadership over events in Ukraine. These smart sanctions, precisely targeting specific influencers, are distinct from the more generic and less effective sanctions introduced at the same time by, for example, the European Union (EU).

20. Peter L. Fitzgerald, "Smarter Smart Sanctions," *International Studies Review*, Vol. 26, 2007, p. 37.

21. Keene, *Threat Finance*, p. 194.

22. Emanuel Strauss, *Concise Dictionary of European Proverbs,* New York and Abingdon, UK: Routledge, 1998.

23. *Hawala* is one of many informal money transfer systems in the world, collectively known as Informal Value Transfer Systems (IVTS). IVTS is a trust-based system used to transfer funds across

countries and continents. In addition, alternative terminologies such as *hawala, hundi, fei ch'ien,* and *phoe kuan* are used, depending on the geographic location and the ethnic group associated with the system. *Hawala* is a term that originated in India and is associated with trust, reference, or exchange.

24. P. M. Jost and H. S. Sandhu, "The *Hawala* Alternative Remittance System and Its Role in Money Laundering," Interpol General Secretariat H.S, 2000.

25. Nikos Passas, "Informal Value Transfer Systems and Criminal Organizations: A Study into So-Called Underground Banking Networks," Boston, MA: Northeastern University, 1999, p. 9.

26. A *Hawaladar* is the *Hawala* agent.

27. FinCen, "Informal Value Transfer Systems," *FinCen Advisory*, United States Department of the Treasury Financial Crimes Enforcement Network Advisory Issue 33, 2003, p. 2.

28. Shima D. Keene, "Terrorism and the Internet: A Double Edged Sword," *Journal of Money Laundering Control*, Vol. 14, No. 4, 2011, p. 359.

29. F. N. Baldwin, "The Financing of Terror in the Age of the Internet: Wilful Blindness, Greed or a Political Statement?" *Journal of Money Laundering Control*, Vol. 8, No. 2, 2004, p. 127.

30. Barry A. K. Rider, "Law: The War on Terror and Crime and the Offshore Centres: The 'New' Perspective?" in Donato Masciandaro, ed., *Global Financial Crime: Terrorism, Money Laundering and Offshore Centres*, Farnham, Surrey, UK: Ashgate Publishing, 2004, p. 92.

31. Keene, *Threat Finance.*

32. Michelle Gallant, "Promise and Perils: The Making of Global Money Laundering, Terrorist Finance Norms," *Journal of Money Laundering Control*, Vol. 13, No. 1, 2010, p. 175.

33. Petrus C. van Duyne, Melvin R. J. Soudijn, "Hot Money, Hot Stones and Hot Air: Crime-Money Threat, Real Estate and Real Concern," *Journal of Money Laundering Control*, Vol. 12, No. 2, 2009, p. 173.

34. G. Merlonghi, "Fighting Financial Crime in the Age of Electronic Money: Opportunities and Limitations," *Journal of Money Laundering Control*, Vol. 13, No. 3, 2010, p. 202.

35. Jeffrey Simser, "Money Laundering and Asset Cloaking Techniques," *Journal of Money Laundering Control*, Vol. 11, No. 1, 2008, p. 15.

36. Loretta Napoleoni, *Modern Jihad: Tracing the Dollars behind the Terror Networks*, London, UK: Pluto Press, 2004, p. 170.

www.ingramcontent.com/pod-product-compliance
Lightning Source LLC
Chambersburg PA
CBHW071142280526
45787CB00003B/1372